IZZY'S
TRASH MOUNTAIN
MYSTERY

Debra Smalley

This book belongs to:

FRANCESCA

IZZY'S
TRASH MOUNTAIN MYSTERY
Debra Smalley

Published By: Debra Smalley
Illustrations By: Riley Knight

Because of the dynamic nature of the Internet, any web addresses or links contained in this book may have changed since publication and may no longer be valid.

ISBN: 9798767850839

To contact the author, Debra Smalley, please email her at:
debra@trashmountainmystery.com

For Press Inquiries, please email:
press@trashmountainmystery.com

To learn more about the book and author, please visit:
www.trashmountainmystery.com

DEDICATION

This book is dedicated to my grandson, Izzy, who inspires me every day.

When Izzy sees his grandmother,
he calls her Gram D.
They are happy to be together
as you can see.

When Izzy's mommy and daddy go away
for a night or a day,
Gram D stays over and they love to play.

Izzy and Gram D laugh on a chair, while doggy Evie pulls and shakes her blanket in the air.

Izzy, Gram D and Evie
pick flowers, jump up
and down on leaves
and look closely at bees.

When it gets dark outside,
Gram D fills the tub with bubbles.
Then Izzy is off to bed
with lots of cuddles and snuggles.

Izzy falls asleep and has a dream.

In his dream, he hears a loud BOOM.
Then Gram D comes into his room,

"Izzy, come see
the pile of trash near the big tree!"

Izzy and Gram D look out the window
at a mountain of papers, glass
and lots of other trash.

"It's a giant Trash Mountain!"
exclaimed Izzy.

"What happened here?
How did this all appear?"
asked Gram D.

"Let's call my friends: Jazmin, Lucia, Matthew and Ky. They live nearby," said Izzy.

The friends come and see Trash Mountain piled high.

"Izzy, what can we do?" asked Matthew.

"This Trash Mountain needs to go away. It is not a healthy or safe place to play!" exclaimed Izzy.

"This mess makes me sad,"
said Izzy.
"You learned magic from your Dad,"
said Gram D.

Izzy lifts his magic light saber and says,

"I know what to say!

Abracadabra! Hocus Pocus!
Make all this go away!"

All of a sudden there is
smoke, thunder and lightning.

When the smoke clears,
the Superheroes appear.

"I'm Rita Cycle,"
said the girl dressed in a blue tutu.
With a pink heart on her sleeve,
she cleans up with a mighty breeze!

"I'm Trasher," said the blue boy.
"I have superpowers!
When I count to three,
you will see!"

Rita said, "This mess needs to go!"
The recycled trash spins so fast!
In the bubble, it's packed!

All the recyclables spin
into a big blue bin.

Then off it goes to the center
for a big recycling adventure.

Trash at the recycle center
is washed and mashed.
The cans, books and plastic
all turn into different things.
It's fantastic!

Where to put what's left
of this unrecyclable mess?

"One, two, three," said Trasher.

Trasher's eyes begin to blink,
his arms go up with a loud clink.
Everyone ducks,
as Trasher transforms
into a super blue trash truck.

The kids move back to give
Trasher more room.
Out of the truck comes a giant vacuum,
that sucks up the garbage
and drives to the dump
to throw away garbage in
Trasher's transformer truck.

"Izzy, great to meet you
and your friends," said Rita.

"Now you know
where trash and garbage go.
You can do magic like Trasher and me.
When you pick up paper, you are
recycling."

Izzy opens his eyes. He is surprised.
He wonders what is he doing in bed?
Izzy runs to the window and says,

"Gram D, remember
the big trash mountain that was
out there!
Now it's nowhere!"

"Izzy, it seems you had a wonderful dream, an adventure that was exciting and with lightning," said Gram D.

"Remember, yesterday
you watched the trash truck drive by?
You waved to Tom, the trash guy."

"Trasher and Rita were in my dream.
I want my friends to see
what the superheroes did.
How we can recycle, us kids,"
said Izzy.

"Izzy, let's get a trash bag
and see what we can do.
Maybe you have toys and
clothes that are too small for
you. When we clean up,
you will all be superheroes too!"

Acknowledgments

I would like to acknowledge David, my son, and Chandra, my daughter-in-law, for being a wonderful Dad and Mom to Izzy.

I give gratitude to Catherine Gray, who has always encouraged my writing and is my biggest supporter in life as well as finishing this book.

Thank you, Andrea Quinn, for your guidance, intuitive direction and wisdom on my journey, which has been immeasurable.

To Minda Burr for her incredible Master Writing Class where this book began.

To Marilyn Brown, my mentor since my early 20s, whose life was dedicated to children, by listening, giving them space and guidance to enable their creativity to flourish.

To my loving parents, who supported me by instilling the adventure and love of reading in me as a very young child.

Note to Parents

A fun follow-up could be with an activity like a scavenger hunt. The parent has a prepared list of things around the house that can be recycled or thrown out for the child to find, and then the child puts it in the appropriate bag.

Another fun game is to 'hunt' for a colored bag and then have your child put in their outgrown toys and clothes to make cleaning up more of a game. By putting things in the bag, it helps teach them how cleaning can help them and others. During the activity, praise your child for their great work and tell them you are proud of them for doing this. Then ask them if they feel proud of themselves. It's encouraging for the child to hear and think about this.

This book creates ways of having lots of fun and connection for the parent, the grandparent and child.

Made in the USA
Las Vegas, NV
27 November 2021